Earth Hour

A Lights-Out Event for Our Planet

Nanette Heffernan   Illustrated by Bao Luu

Charlesbridge

All over the world, millions of people use energy, every day, every night.

Energy makes our home
toasty when it's cool.

It cooks the dumpling soup
we ladle into bowls.

Energy helps our ancient heritage shine proud.

It heats the terrace as we dine under the stars.

And it keeps darkness at bay through the long polar nights.

Energy washes the fun and games from our clothes.

When day is done, it warms our bath
as we *splash, splash, splash.*

Energy is a wonderful resource from Earth—
a gift from nature we respect and conserve.

This is why, on a Saturday night, at
8:30 sharp, near the equinox in March . . .

. . . on every continent,

in quiet celebration

millions join together

to turn out their lights.

From an opera house

to a great wall . . .

...to a resting site, magnificent,

and four hundred feet high.

Light after light goes dark around us.

Yet this one hour a year isn't enough.

Every light counts, every day, every night,

whether tiny or giant, bright or dim.

Alone we are one . . . .

... but together we have power.

United, we are Earth Hour.

MORE ABOUT EARTH HOUR

Earth Hour is celebrated on all seven continents, in almost every country. Millions flip their switch during this annual lights-out celebration that unites people across our planet. What started in 2007 as a tiny creative idea in Sydney, Australia, has blossomed into a global movement that is now managed by the World Wildlife Fund for Nature (WWF). On a Saturday night near the equinox in March, all over the world, at 8:30 p.m. local time, lights fade to black for this special event. In Sydney, homes and restaurants—and even the famous Sydney Opera House—turn out their lights. An hour later Tokyo goes dark. Two hours later it's Beijing's turn. Thousands of famous monuments, from the Taj Mahal to the Eiffel Tower to the Golden Gate Bridge, unplug for the event.

BUT WHY?

We turn off our lights as a pledge to live more sustainably and conserve energy—not just during Earth Hour but during every hour and every day throughout the year. Most energy today comes from burning fossil fuels such as coal, oil, and gas. Making electricity from fossil fuels puts more pollution into the air. The pollution generated from all these energy sources is primarily greenhouse gases. Heat gets trapped close to Earth's surface by these greenhouse gases, similar to the way a car parked in the sun with its windows closed traps heat inside of it. Record temperatures and an increase in these gases have led scientists on every continent to agree that our planet is heating up.

As our planet warms, the weather across each continent is affected. Scientists call this climate change. Due to warmer weather, some areas now get more rain, floods, and hurricanes that often damage entire cities. Other areas experience droughts, making it difficult to grow food or to get clean drinking water. Glaciers melt, eradicating the habitats of polar bears and penguins. This also causes oceans to rise and swallow up coastlands. If animals cannot adapt to the climate changes in their habitats, they will have to migrate or they could die off. Even people in some parts of the world may have to find new places to live.

One of the best ways to reduce climate change is to use less energy! We can also reduce pollution by using energy from wind, water, sun, and garbage—all renewable sources of energy that don't create harmful greenhouse gases.

It's important for us to do our part and conserve. We can do this by celebrating Earth Hour in our own way. Snuggle up with milk and cookies, play games by candlelight, or lie under the stars. No matter how we celebrate, there's one thing we have in common: Earth is home to us all. Whether you are two or one hundred and two, you can spend sixty minutes during Earth Hour saving energy and making a pledge to protect our planet year round.

AUTHOR'S NOTE

Several years ago I was driving home at night across the Golden Gate Bridge in San Francisco, California. Suddenly the lights on the bridge went out. I thought there had been a power outage. Later I learned that the bridge had gone dark in honor of Earth Hour. I was an instant fan and supporter of this movement to recognize the energy we use. I visited www.earthhour.org to learn everything I could about this amazing event. The more I learned, the more I wanted to encourage others to join. Exactly one year later I went back to the Golden Gate Bridge. When the lights went out at 8:30 sharp, I stood in the dark and made my pledge: "I will share this event with one million people," I said to myself. That night the first draft of the book you are holding was born. Have you made an Earth Hour pledge? If so, thank you; I'm honored that we share this planet. My hope is that we will all make a pledge and all share it with the world at www.earthhourthebook.com.

THANK YOU, AND HAPPY EARTH HOUR!

To Nikolai, Max, and Anie—the lights of my life!
—N. H.

I would like to dedicate this book to you—the reader. Thank
you for being part of my dream of working as an illustrator.
—B. L.

Text copyright © 2020 by Nanette Heffernan
Illustrations copyright © 2020 by Bao Luu
All rights reserved, including the right of reproduction in whole or in
part in any form. Charlesbridge and colophon are registered trademarks
of Charlesbridge Publishing, Inc.

Published by Charlesbridge, 85 Main Street, Watertown, MA 02472
(617) 926-0329 • www.charlesbridge.com

At the time of publication, all URLs printed in this book were
accurate and active. Charlesbridge, the author, and the illustrator
are not responsible for the content or accessibility of any website.

Illustrations created using Adobe Photoshop on a Wacom Cintiq
Display type set in Bombay Blue by David Kerkhoff
Text type set in Hank BT by Bitstream Inc.
Color separations by Colourscan Print Co Pte Ltd, Singapore
Printed by 1010 Printing International Limited in Huizhou, Guangdong, China
Production supervision by Brian G. Walker
Designed by Joyce White and Susan Mallory Sherman

Library of Congress Cataloging-in-Publication Data
Names: Heffernan, Nanette, author. | Luu, Bao, illustrator.
Title: Earth hour: a lights-out event for our planet / Nanette Heffernan;
    illustrated by Bao Luu.
Description: Watertown, MA: Charlesbridge, [2020]
Identifiers: LCCN 2018052240 (print) | LCCN 2019000498 (ebook) |
    ISBN 9781632896858 (ebook) | ISBN 9781632896865 (ebook pdf) |
    ISBN 9781580899420 (reinforced for library use)
Subjects: LCSH: Energy conservation—Juvenile literature. | Climatic
    changes—Social aspects—Juvenile literature. | Special events—
    Juvenile literature.
Classification: LCC TJ163.35 (ebook) | LCC TJ163.35 .H44 2020 (print) |
    DDC 333.791/6—dc23
LC record available at https://lccn.loc.gov/2018052240

Printed in China
(hc) 10 9 8 7 6 5 4 3 2 1